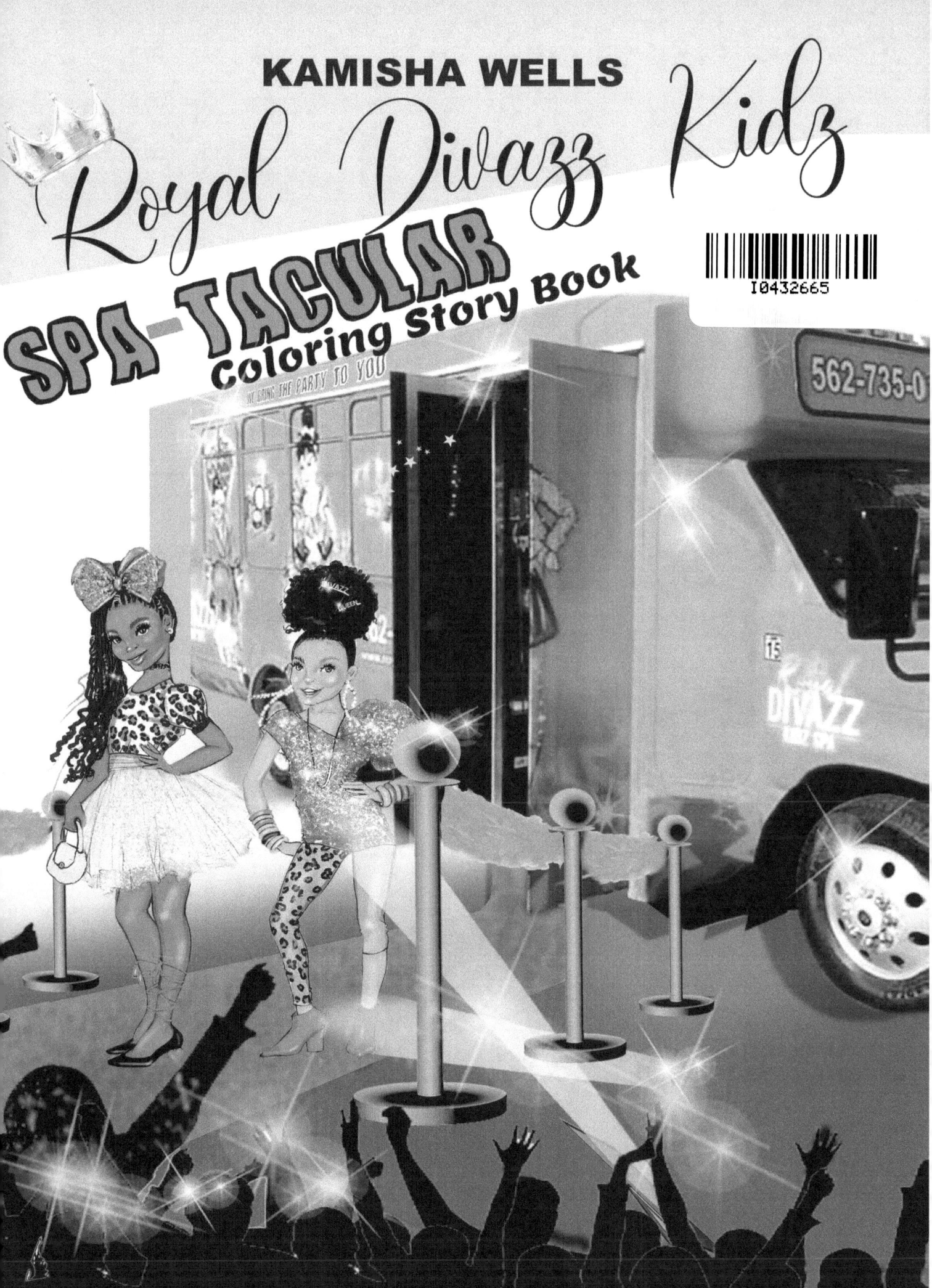

Royal Divazz Kidz Spa-Tacular Coloring Story Book
All Rights Reserved.
Copyright © 2020 Kamisha Wells
v1.0

This is a work of fiction. The events and characters described herein are imaginary and are not intended to refer to specific places or living persons. The opinions expressed in this manuscript are solely the opinions of the author and do not represent the opinions or thoughts of the publisher. The author has represented and warranted full ownership and/or legal right to publish all the materials in this book.

This book may not be reproduced, transmitted, or stored in whole or in part by any means, including graphic, electronic, or mechanical without the express written consent of the publisher except in the case of brief quotations embodied in critical articles and reviews.

Outskirts Press, Inc.
http://www.outskirtspress.com

ISBN: 978-1-9772-2726-3

Cover Photo © 2020 Kamisha Wells. All rights reserved - used with permission.

· Outskirts Press and the "OP" logo are trademarks belonging to Outskirts Press, Inc.

PRINTED IN THE UNITED STATES OF AMERICA

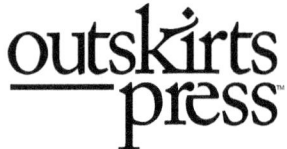

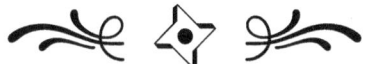

This Book Belongs to:

_____

Royal Spa

Mom! Mom! The bus Is Here!! The Bus Is Here!! My friends and I ran outside, the royal hostess came off the Bus and told us to line up on the Runway, OMG!! The runway is pink with sparkles and boa feathers Crowd control, as we enter the spa bus, ME!! FIRST IM THE BIRTHDAY GIRL!! I received my spa robe, spa slippers, sash and princess crown, my friends received there spa robes, and spa slippers, ALL I COULD DO IS LOOK AROUND AT HOW AMAZING AND BEAUTIFUL EVERYTHING IS, I feel like Royalty, the hostess had all of us sit down, and hold our heads back so they can apply facemask and cucumber eyes.

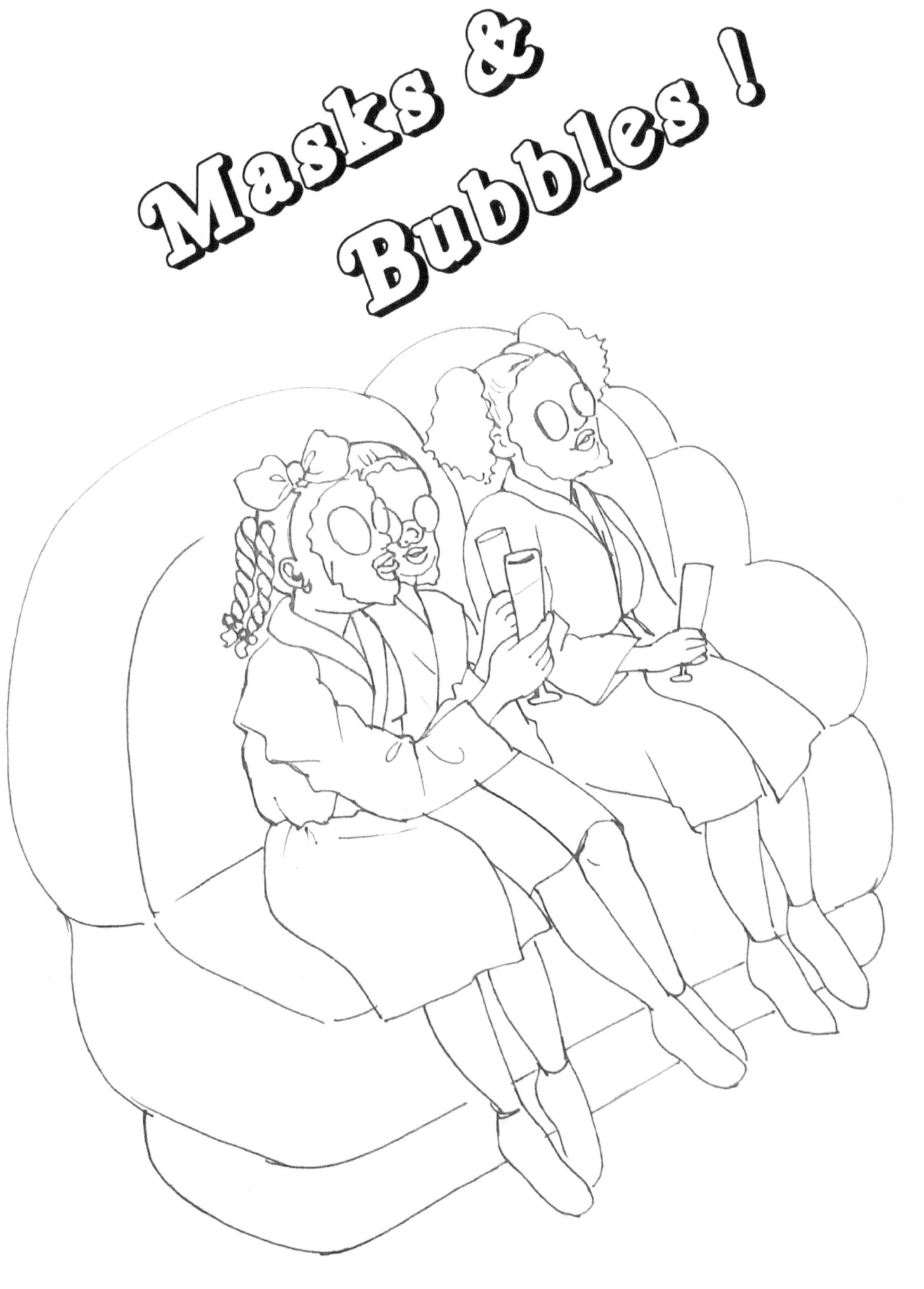

LOL & Unicorn Paint Party

Dad knows how much I love to paint, but he said no arts and crafts today sweetie, I must work! Let's go take a walk on the beach for some fresh air. as we were walking up to the beach, I notice a big pink spa bus with purple tents, purple and pink chairs and as I get closer, I see a LOL surprise doll and unicorn princess dancing wearing a paint apron! Then I notice a colorful unicorn horse a real horse!! riding kids around the beach, I see a couple of my friends sitting at the table with stencils, paint brushes and aprons on. I looked up at my dad ran over very quickly to my friends, hugging them than ran and jumped on the unicorn horse riding away "Yelling" Dad this is amazing I will never forget this day.

Beach and Paint !

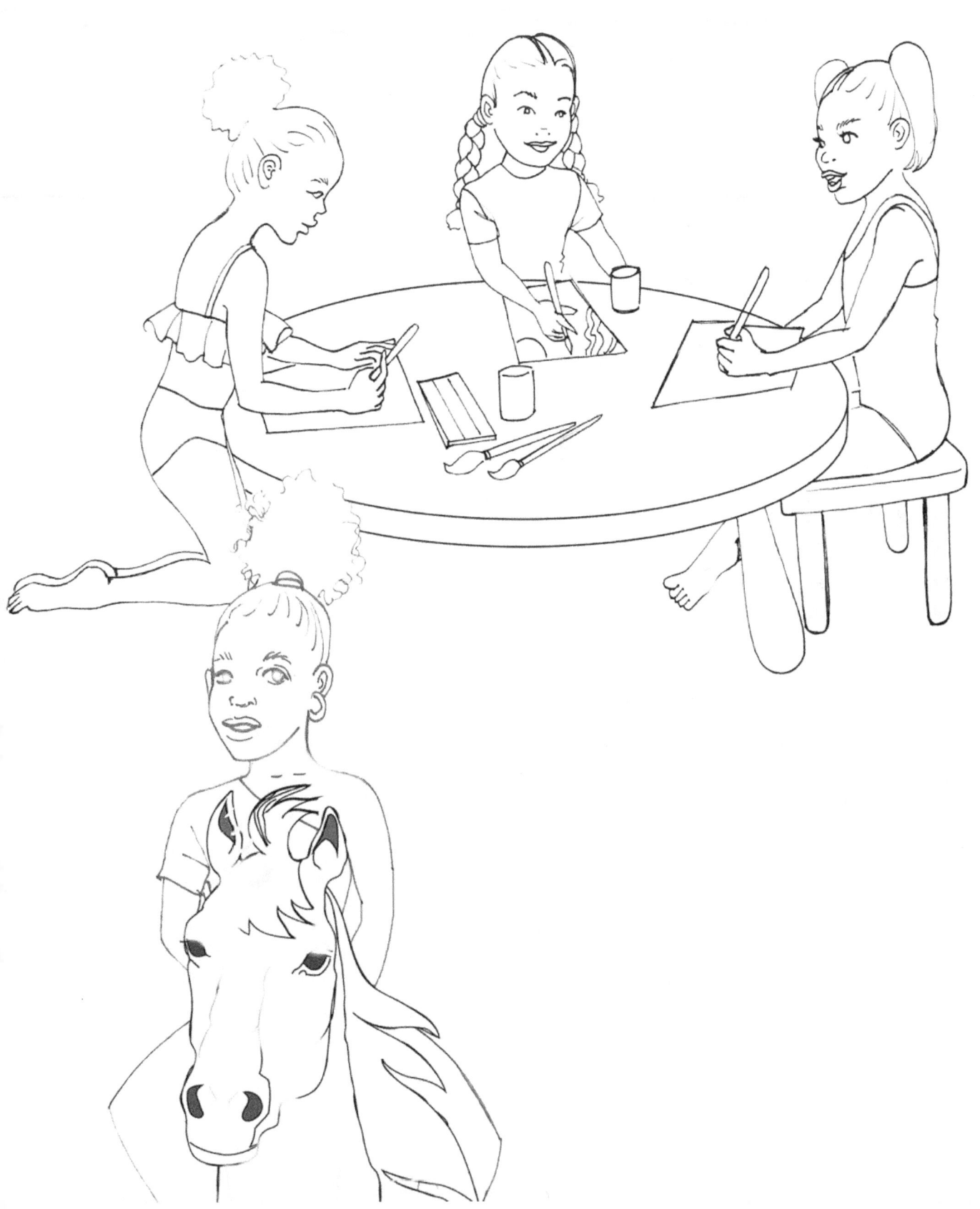

Teatime with Princess

It's my Birthday!! Its finally here!! I'm here at the park, with my sisters and close friends, I'm so Excited, Grandma booked Royal Divazz Kidz Spa, it's so magical, the tea tables are setup outside the spa bus with fancy tea drinks, sandwich with the edges cut off, fruit bowls, sugar cookies, each chair had assigned name tags, with foot spa bowls with rose peddles in each one. tea hats, tea gloves, tea dresses and a beautiful princess sitting at our tea table sipping on tea!! The Royal Princess taught us etiquette skills, table manners, we did activities than we danced to our favorite Princess song.

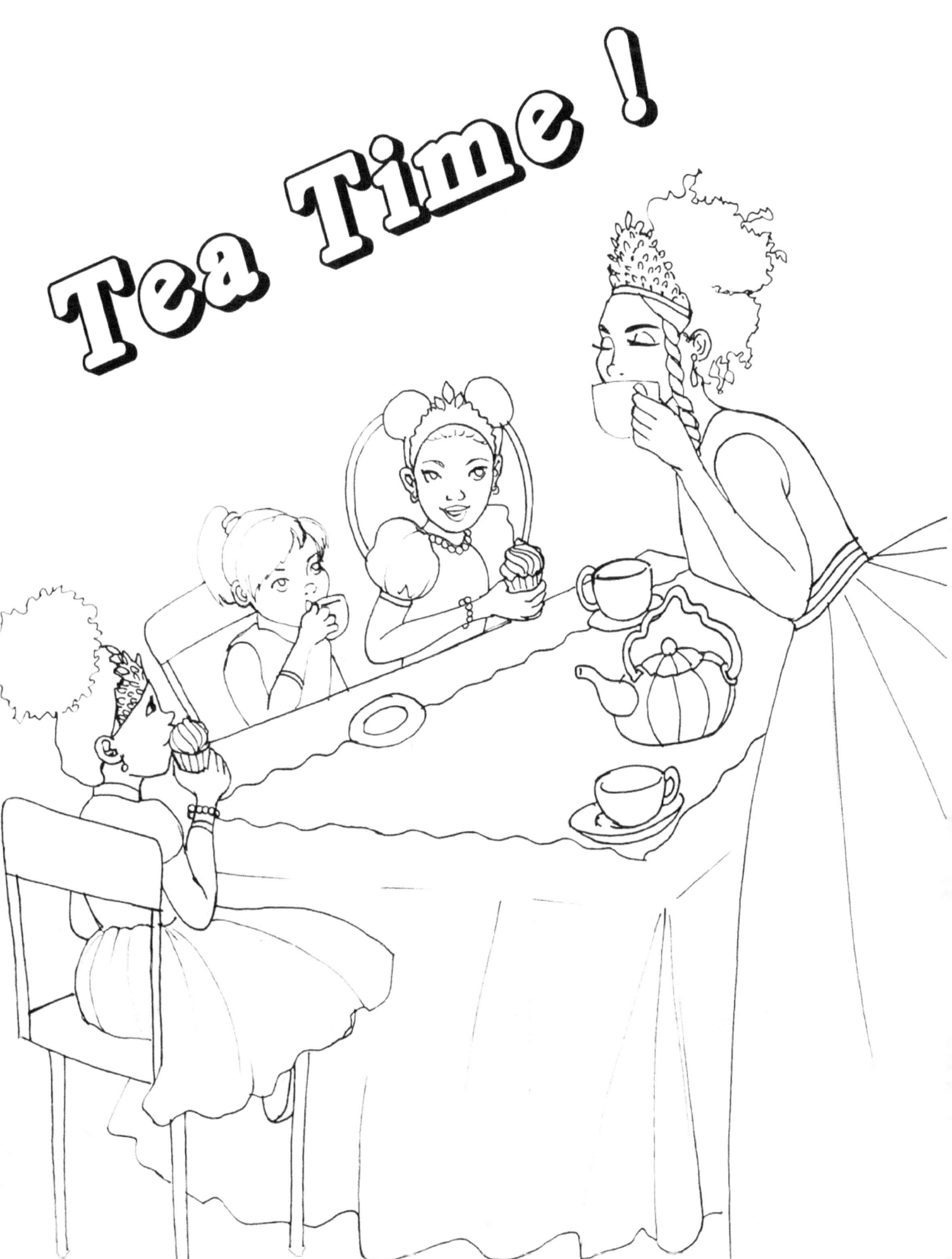

Spa Movie Night

The new Mermaid movie is out today, but Uncle Jeremiah said all the tickets are sold out at every theater. Uncle what are we going to do now "in my sad voice" I have been waiting forever to see my favorite movie. Uncle pondered hummmmm I will keep searching. 5 minutes later...Wait!!!! There's a spa party bus that has a movie night package let's give them a call. (562)735-0110 YESS they are fitting us in last minute. I didn't know what to expect but when they arrived everything was taken care of. when they say they bring the party to you they bring the party to you. they setup an inflatable outdoor movie screen with a projector and big DJ speakers. All in the comfort of my backyard with popcorn and cotton candy machines. My niece got the chance to watch her favorite movie after all.

Movie Night !

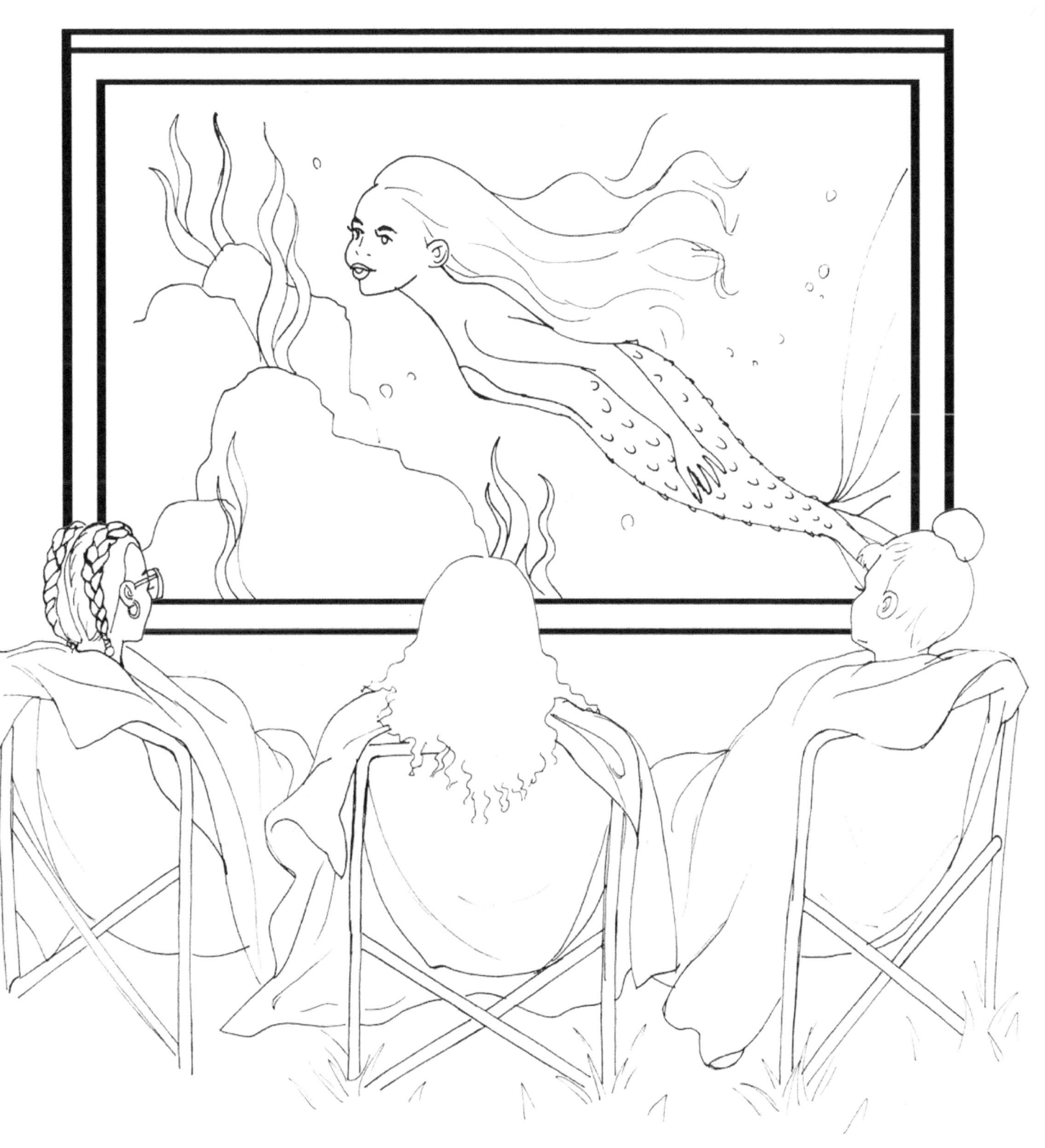

Royal All Abilities Spa

The phone rings, could your company Royal Divazz please sponsor our special needs cheerleading team? Yes, we would be honored to, we are also parents of two young boys with Autism. As the bus arrived on the football field the girl's faces were priceless. As they walk into the spa bus with big smiles from ear to ear dancing to the music as they set down to get pampered by are amazing royal hostess. Once they finished getting pampered and having a mini makeover done, they modeled their diva dresses with accessories down, our fashion runway to show their coaches and families what they have been doing on the spa bus. After an evening of fun laughter, pampering and dancing our royal hostess passed out custom royal gift bags fit for each girl.

Some Me Time !

Mommy and Me

Mom wanted to do something special today with just us girls. No special occasion a girl's spa day. As the Royal Divazz Spa bus arrived at our house, the hostess rolled out the red carpet with rose petals to walk on before entering the bus. As we walked in the hostess were standing there with our spa robes, slippers and a glass of apple cider. While receiving our mini pedicures we sing karaoke and made mother and daughter matching beaded bracelets. Then we picked each other accessories, wigs, boa feathers and dresses off the diva rack to model for the royal fashion show. We had an awesome time modeling and making fun of each other crazy outfits and funny wig. We took pictures with the photo props and made DIY perfume and lip-gloss outside the spa bus and a lifetime of memories.

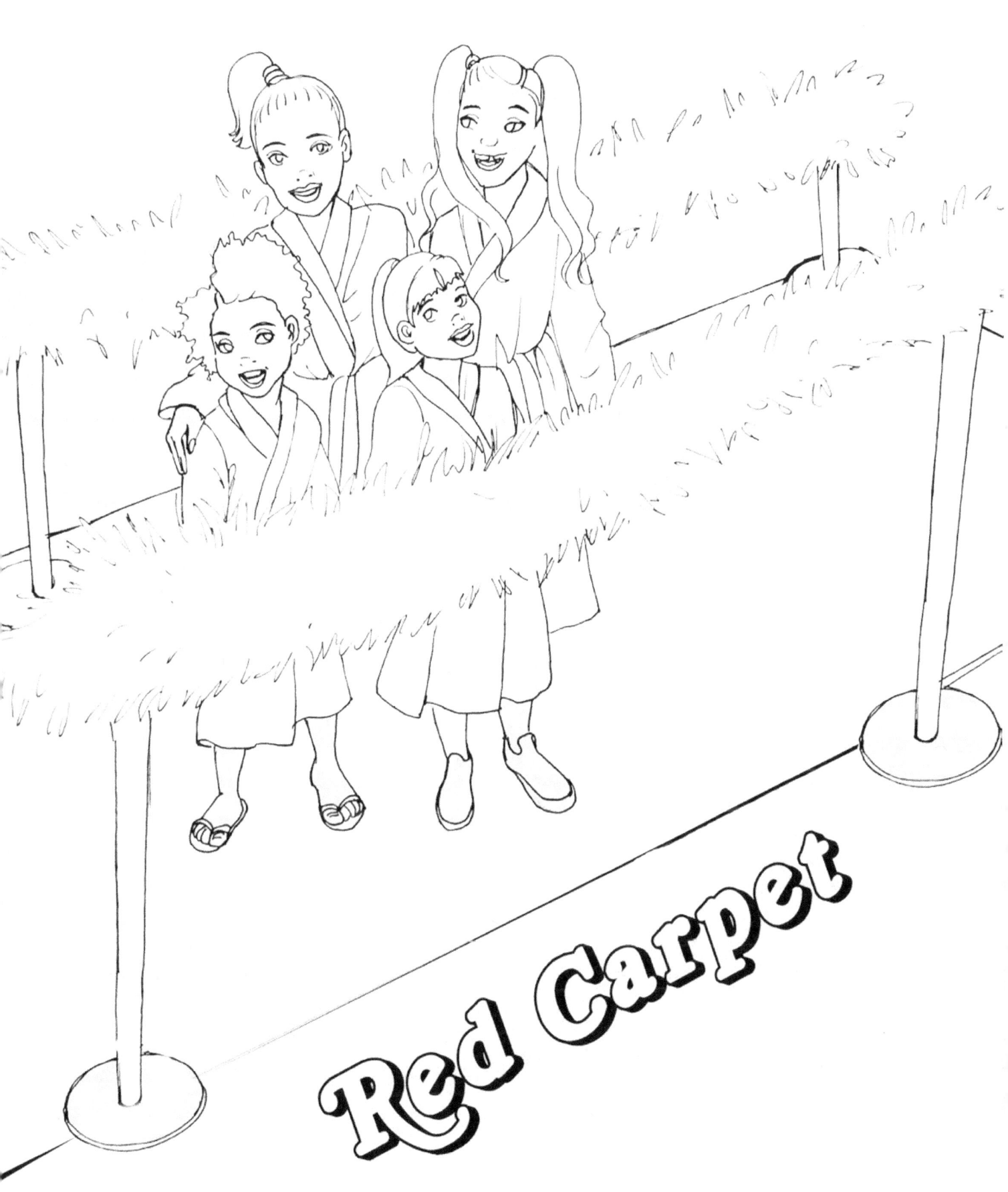

Community Summer Fun

Giving back to our community is an honor and humbling experience to be a part of. We had the opportunity to join organizations and pamper the kids in the community at the back to school, thanksgiving, Christmas events, Christmas parades, foster care events and more...

Bus party !

Princess Aaliyah & Princess A'mora

Every girl pretends she is a princess at one point, Aaliyah and A'mora are the princesses you see on our spa bus. The best thing about making memories is making them with each one of you. Embrace your inner princess. Bold is beautiful see you at your next event.

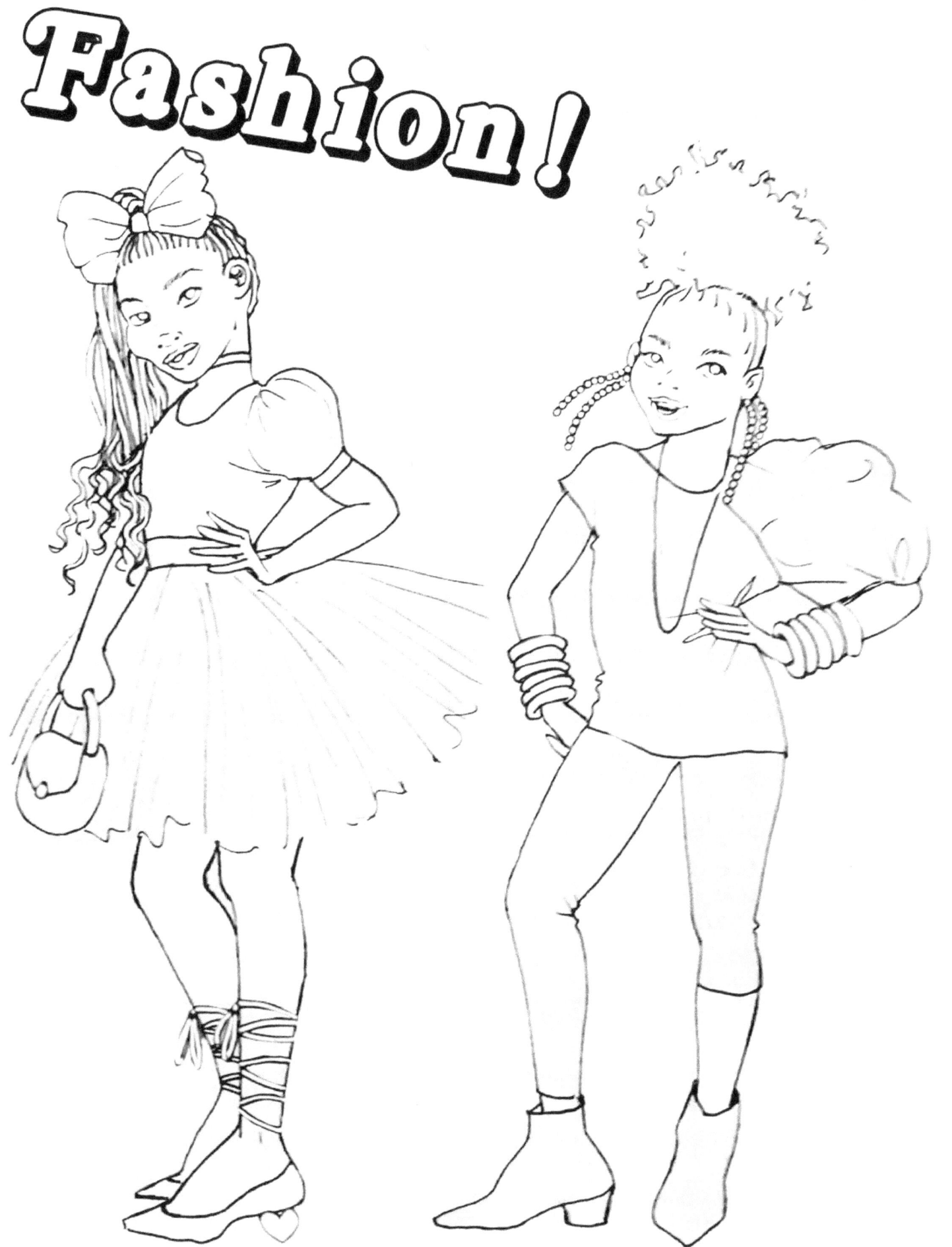

Crafting with School

The principle called and asked if Royal Divazz could be a part of their school Science event. The bus arrived and parked on the school playground and setup six science slime actives tables with microscopes and DIY volcano science slime and much more. All reserved teachers and children each received a white science lab jacket, science googles and gloves. After the DIY science actives, the boys and girls each received a Royal Divazz Certificate of accomplishment and the first-place winner received a Royal Diva Trophy.

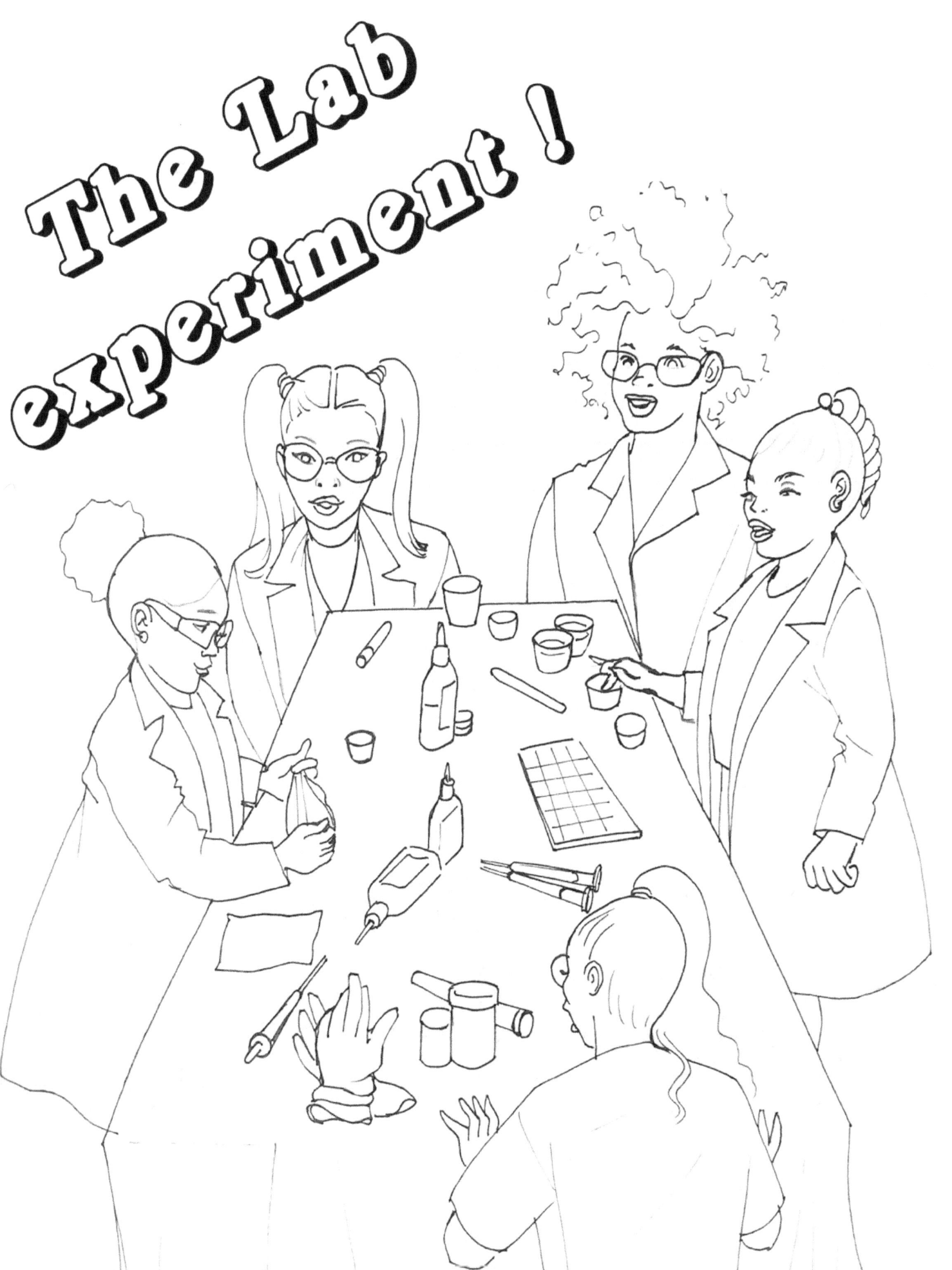

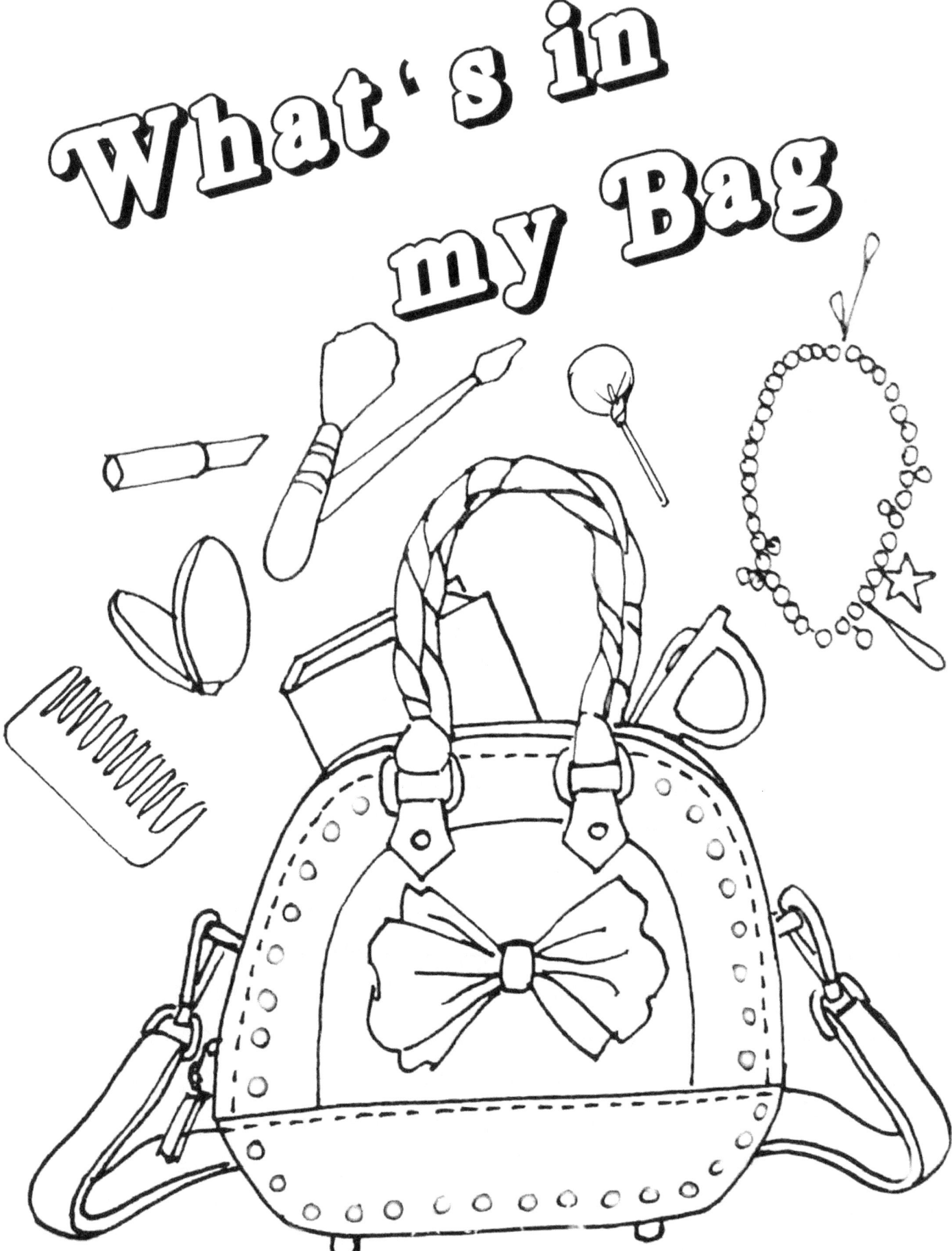

Royal Spa Party !

```
H D R F T Q G M W G O B I Q C U G
F H U U R S L D G Y S C U J R Q T
Z W K A Y O E M O V L Q N Z E P X
U F C G Y A W V R K H I K E A V E
P H K C Y K U I V X Y O N G M G J
Q L F E E N E H Y G B V K X A E Y
M A R O Z Y D H P Y X X F Q S L L
S H A M P O O Y N A I L N H S V R
L O T I O N V J G G M M S P A S X
L O J Y W C M A S K Y P C V G F C
B F Q P N M A N I C U R E L E Z S
D S C E J N O W A M Y Z N Q K L Y
D L O U B A G H L S L T C I T F G
O F L U P E D I C U R E Z V F O F
I H O H S Z G A L W D V X I Z O U
P O L I S H I R E L A X X T Q T N
E E J M K W A W C B U B B L E S S
```

Lotion	Gel	Cream	Bubbles
Foot	Fun	Manicure	Mask
Massage	Nail	Pedicure	Polish
Relax	Shampoo	Soak	Spa

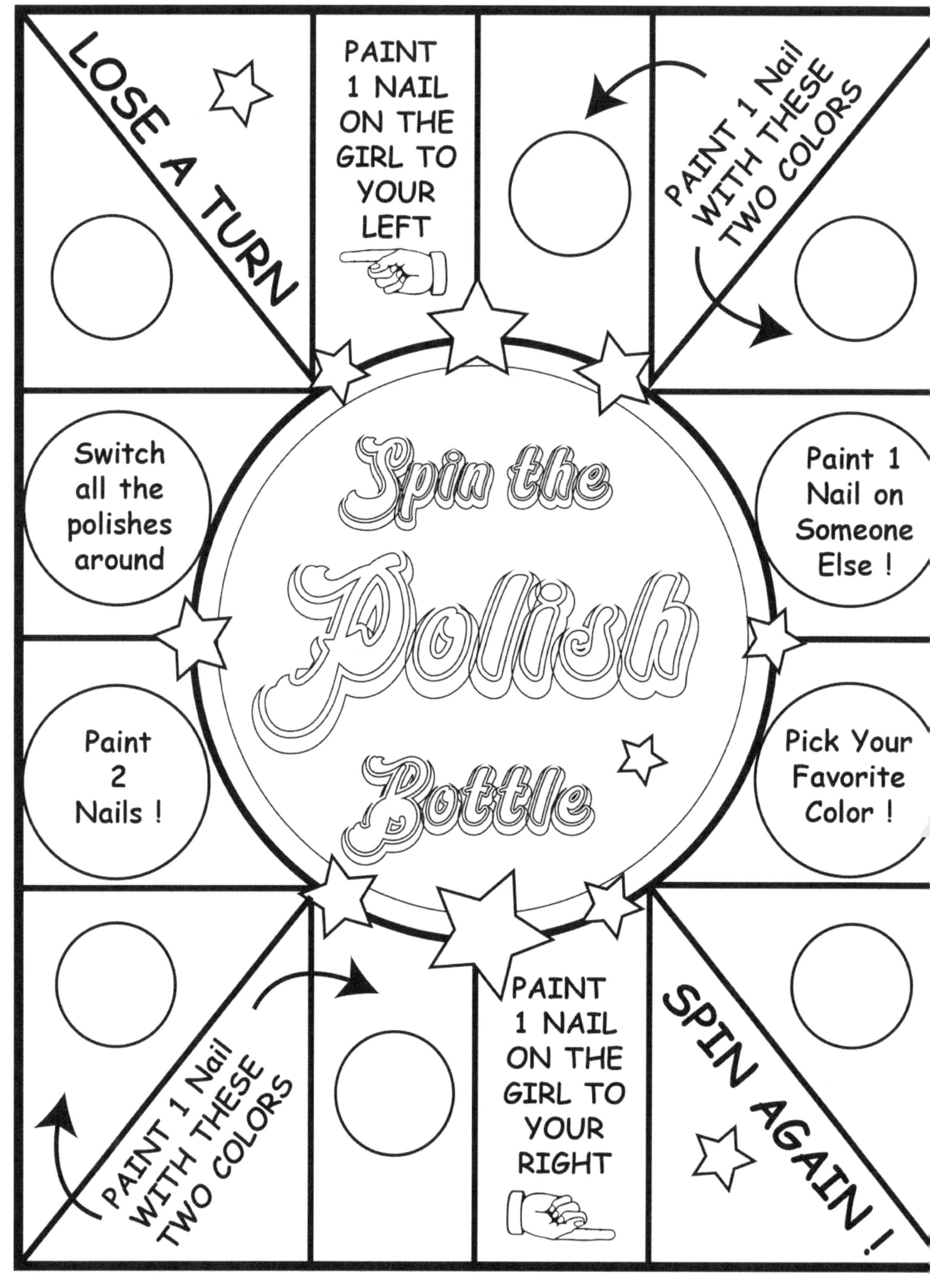

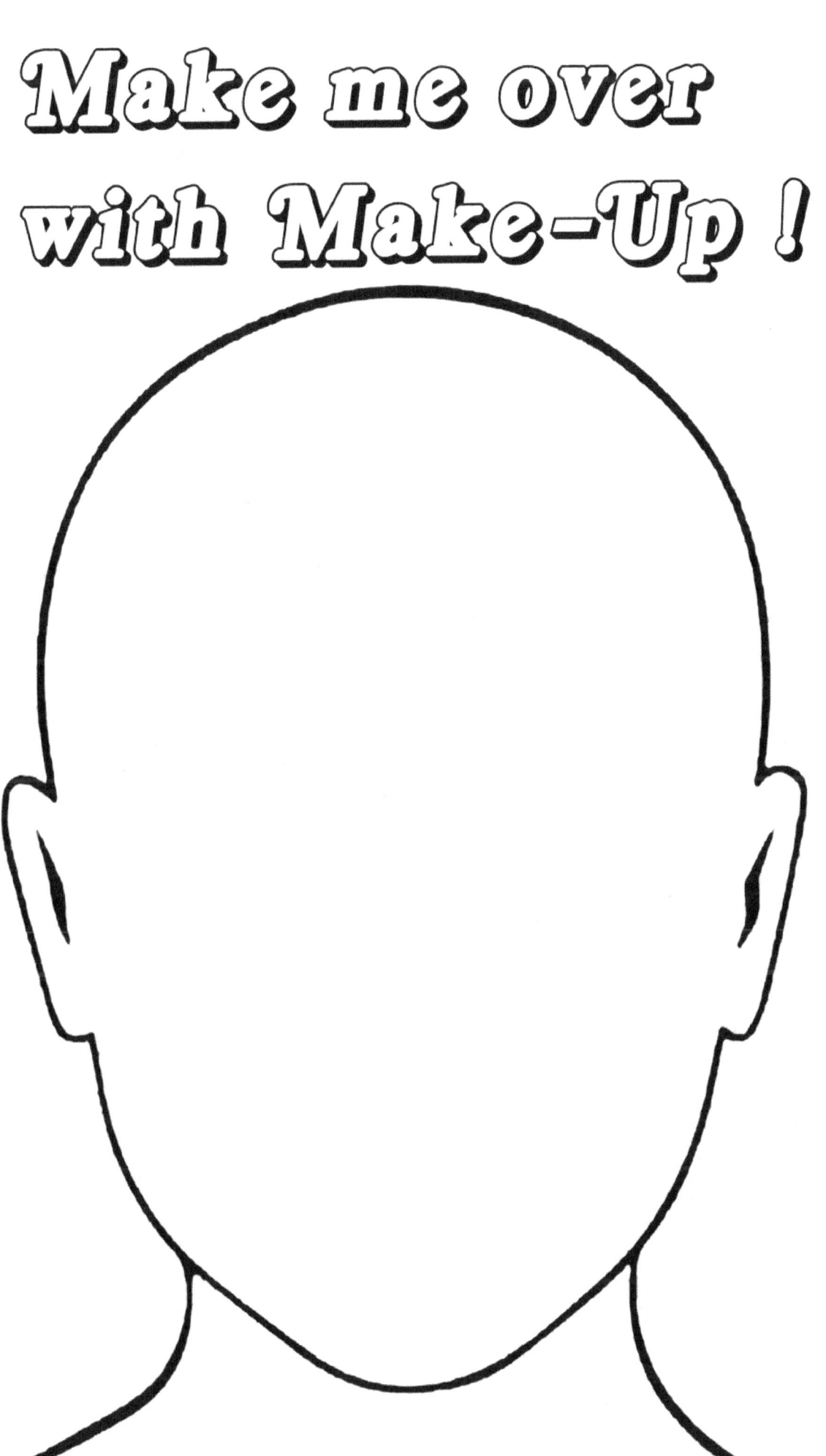

ROYAL DIVAZZ KIDZ MOBILE SPA LLC, is an upscale mobile spa party bus that specializes in pampering young princesses ages 3-14 to look and feel their absolute best! We are known for being experts in the field who create customized parties with the best services available to make your princess feel like royalty.

We provide a safe and fun environment for birthdays, group playdates, and all other special events. Our outgoing and skilled party hostess are here to pamper, enhance and encourage girls to feel good about themselves, and most of all provide them with the most magical celebration of their dreams.

Our Mission is to inspire young ladies to celebrate their beauty and uniqueness we encourage them to feel like a princess while being showered in glitter. Royal Divazz Kidz Mobile Spa Parties are worthwhile because we provide youth leadership, motivation, mentoring, relaxation. Our job is to make sure we leave these young ladies feeling happy, beautiful, encouraged, inspired, strong and most of all empowered. We teach them the importance of self-care, hygiene and self-esteem.

www.royaldivazzspa.com

(562)735-0110

www.ingramcontent.com/pod-product-compliance
Lightning Source LLC
Chambersburg PA
CBHW062209220526
45470CB00009B/2985